CARVING FACIAL EXPRESSIONS

Carving

FACIAL EXPRESSIONS

Ian Norbury

LINDEN PUBLISHING

FRESNO, CALIFORNIA

CARVING FACIAL EXPRESSIONS
by
Ian Norbury

456789

ISBN: 0-941936-43-0

Library of Congress Cataloging in Publication Information

Norbury, Ian.
    Carving facial expressions / Ian Norbury.
            p.   cm.
    ISBN o-941936-43-0
    1. Wood-carving—Technique. 2. Facial expression in art. 3. Face
in art. I. Title
TT199.7.N65   1997
736'.4—dc21
                                                        97-36116
                                                          CIP

© 1997 Ian Norbury
Printed in the United States of America

LINDEN PUBLISHING INC
2006 S. MARY
FRESNO, CA 93721
www.lindenpub.com
800-345-4447

CONTENTS

Books by the same author

Fundamentals of Figure Carving
Techniques of Creative Woodcarving
Projects for Creative Woodcarving
Relief Woodcarving & Lettering

In preparation

The Complete Guide to Woodcarving
Fundamentals of Animal Carving

Acknowledgements

I would like to thank Pippa Dunn, James Norbury, Jayne Norbury, Alex Penning, Robert Penning, Tony Penning and Adrian Robinson for their patience as models; Mr and Mrs M. Boers, Mr and Mrs Brewer, Mr and Mrs H. Brock, Mr and Mrs A.E. Brookes, Mr P. Brooking, Mr and Mrs B. Channin, Mr and Mrs S. Channing-Williams, Mr and Mrs T. Edgeworth, Mr and Mrs S. Ellis, Mr and Mrs S. Golding, Mr J. Homer, Mr and Mrs K. Kelly, Mr D. Martin, Mr and Mrs B. Mosley, Mr and Mrs M. Perry, Mr and Mrs R. Stewart, Mr and Mrs W. van Draat, Mr and Mrs R.G. Vincent, Mr and Mrs B. White, Mr D.C.C. Wilson, Mr and Mrs M. Winlow, for permitting their sculptures to be illustrated.

1

INTRODUCTION

There are few things in the world more imbued with fascination, intrigue, mystery, mythology — the list would be endless — than the human face and the meaning behind the expressions that pass across it.

The concept, held for thousands of years, that man was the most perfect creation of nature is perhaps not as prevalent today, but the supreme complexity and subtlety of the human brain are probably more appreciated and understood than ever before.

Neurology can explain many of the minute physical functions of the brain and psychology is able to analyse the motivation for man's behaviour. Most if not all of these cerebral activities manifest themselves in physical activity ranging from the smallest increase in heartbeat or perspiration to explosions of energy such as running or fighting. These manifestations are invariably accompanied by muscular activity in the face resulting in changes of what are commonly called 'facial expressions'. 'Facial expressions', in the vast majority of people, are the visible display of invisible, mental and physical processes such as pain, concentration or amusement. Of course, the facial muscles are controllable except in certain situations such as sneezing or vomiting, and some people make it their business to exercise a high

degree of control, for example card players and actors. Most people only control their expressions under special circumstances, at a funeral perhaps, and usually not very well. These facial expressions are fairly universal, though not completely so. For instance, in some countries raising the eyebrow accompanied by clocking the tongue indicates a negative decision, whereas elsewhere in the world it suggests disdain or disapproval.

However, in this book we are not concerned with the customs that may prevail in different parts of the world, but with the 'road signs' that are commonly understood in the western world.

Different people display these facial expressions to different degree — some are said to have a 'mobile face', or an 'expressive face', and so on. The skeletal and muscular structure of each individual varies or reacts differently. By constant use certain muscular reactions or expressions become more strongly ingrained in an individual's features; a permanently raised 'quizzical' eyebrow or a 'disapproving' downturned mouth. As time goes by these features become virtually permanent fixtures on a person's face, they come to be regarded as 'characteristic features', they are supposed to indicate the 'character' of the person. In the past, the pseudo-science of physiognomy believed absolutely that a person's nature and mental state could be accurately deduced by measuring their facial features, just as phrenology maintained that it could by mapping the lumps and bumps on the skull. I think that reading 'character' from the lines and wrinkles on someone's face is just about as fallacious as physiognomy and phrenology.

However, from the point of view of artists, a bad person has always had a nasty face and a happy person is one with laughter lines. The purpose of this book is fourfold: first, to explain briefly and as non-technically as possible how the facial expressions are created by muscular activity; second, to give a wide range of illustrations of facial expressions, using different models of different sexes, age and builds, which can be used by carvers as reference material for their own work; third, to give a few working examples of carving these 'expressions', simply and effectively; and finally, to show a range of carved faces by myself and others, which will hopefully inspire the woodcarver to personally explore this fascinating subject.

Most carvers I know, like to create figures; the face and body are interdependent, the face expressing the feelings of the body and the body giving meaning to the expression of the face. A figure with a bland face is only half a figure.

With this in mind it will clearly pay dividends to make a thorough study of the face, its structure and function over a wide range of individuals — young, old, fat, thin, male and female in a great variety of emotional states. Such is the infinite diversity of the face that any book can only provide a tiny sample of the types. It is incumbent on the carver to collect photographs of faces from every source he can to provide his own reference library. Do not be deceived into believing that you can make up a convincing, realistic face from your own imagination without many years of experience. Furthermore, great satisfaction can be obtained from creating a face from sound reference material, thereby achieving an end result that conveys to all the expressions intended, qualified by evidence from nature.

Carvers involved in a wide range of subjects will find this invaluable. Obviously those indulging in the increasingly popular craft of carving caricatures should derive great benefit and their work will improve dramatically, as the stereotyped expressions some of them use are replaced by real ones. Portraits and self-portraits will also be found easier to achieve by understanding the mechanics of the face. Religious figures, fantasy figures, studies of people working or sportsmen, all popular subjects can all benefit from improvement of the facial expression. The fringe benefit is that once you get into faces, it becomes quite a fascinating study, and you will find yourself constantly watching people. If you can bring yourself to make a few little sketches while you are watching, so much the better. Of course, the easiest way is to study your own face. The artist Messerschmit made 47 lead models of his own head, making what he considered to be every possible expression. These are striking, if bizarre pieces, but you will derive great understanding by looking in the mirror and pulling faces. Be careful the wind does not change!

2

THE BASIC
FACE

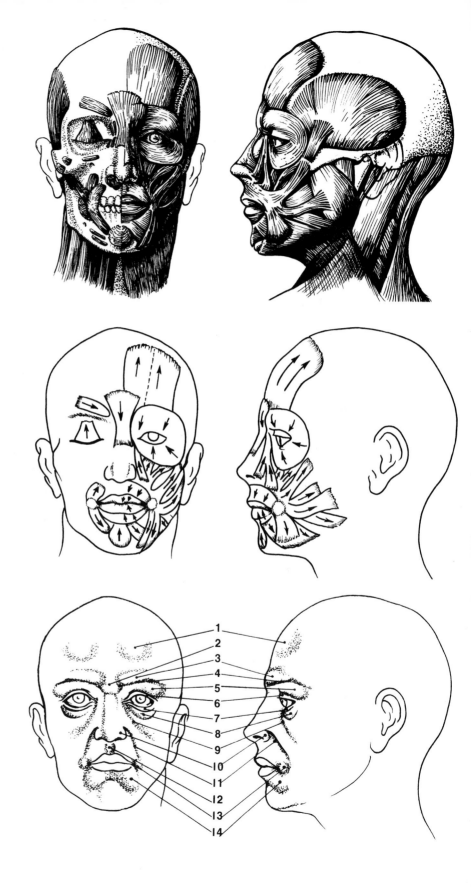

Before we can progress in the carving of expressions it is necessary to establish a basic face, virtually devoid of expression, which we can then use as a point of reference. The drawings in Figs 1 and 2 show a diagrammatic representation of the facial muscles and the way in which they work.

Figs 1–2

Fig. 3   Key:
1. Frontal emminence
2. Glabella
3. Brow ridge
4. Eyebrow
5. Eye cover fold
6. Upper eyelid
7. Lower eyelid
8. Tear bag
9. Infra-orbital furrow
10. Wing of nose
11. Naso-labrial furrow
12. Philtrum
13. Node
14. Pillar of mouth

Study the drawing and photograph in Figs 5 and 6. The face is expressionless — vacant, as we would say — no wrinkles, no frown, no smile. The only features are those formed by permanent physical features, the eyebrows, eyeballs and lids, the infra-orbital furrow, the naso-labial furrow, the pillars of the mouth, the nose, the chin boss. Even some of these shapes are very soft and subtle and can only be perceived by judicious lighting.

It would be very easy for me to carve a large head, say two thirds life size, with hair and other encumbrances well out of the way to facilitate the work. However, long experience of teaching carvers has shown me that most of them are working on a small scale because the figures they carve are quite small. Even on a statue one metre high the head would only be about 15cm (6") tall, and few carvers aspire to that size.

In this example the head is 10cm (4") high which although still quite large for a figure, uses the same basic technique as a smaller one, which are in some ways different from those used on a larger head.

Fig. 5

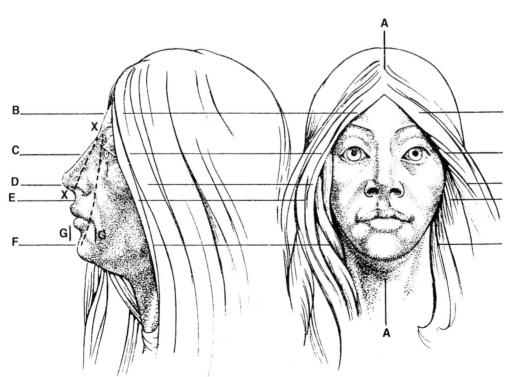

Fig. 6

Measurement becomes less precise with a small scale, a cut of the chisel can alter the face disastrously; edges become perilously thin.

Also in this example, the hair is in the way. This means that the profile can only partially be bandsawn and the front view is only the outline of the hair. This makes accurate bandsawing even more imperative than usual because the bandsawn outline must be used as the reference point for measuring to locate the face.

The block of wood must be planed perfectly square to avoid inaccuracy and the drawing traced on very carefully, using a square around the block to ensure that various points on the two profiles are dead level, as in Fig. 4.

When the block has been bandsawn from both sides, the first move is to draw in the centre line 'A' locating it by measuring from either side. Fig. 6. Then measure outwards from the centre line along the lines 'B', 'C', 'D', 'E' and 'F' to the outline of the front view of the face, carefully drawing this onto the wood. Now measure from the centre to the sides of the nose at the nostrils and at the bridge, drawing the

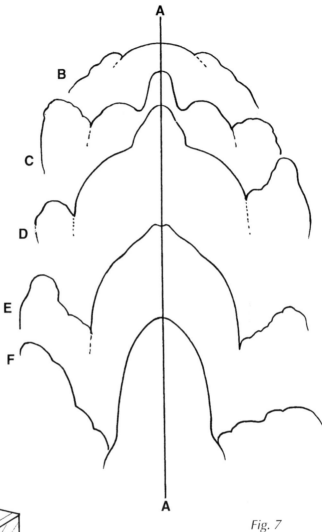

Fig. 7

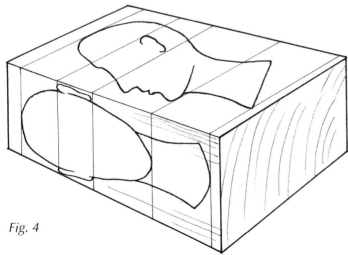

Fig. 4

wedge shape shown in Fig. 8. On the side of the head draw in the line down the length of the nose 'X'. The area either side of the nose can now be cut away, Fig. 9. Redraw the outline of the face. Next draw in the line of the hair running down the chest on the front, and the line of the neck and chest on the side, Fig. 9. The area can be cut away, Fig. 10. The waste areas should be cut and removed neatly and cleanly taking both surfaces square across into a clean square corner. Another area of waste is now removed at the left of the neck, Fig. 10. In Fig. 11 this has gone and the next part is hatched. Cut this away taking care not to cut into the side of the face.

Fig. 8

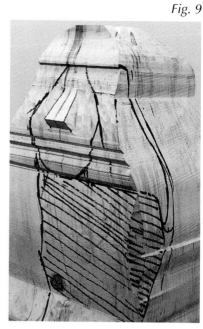

Fig. 9

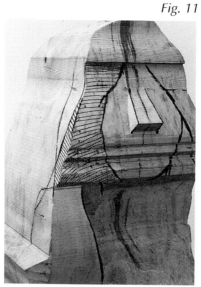

Fig. 10

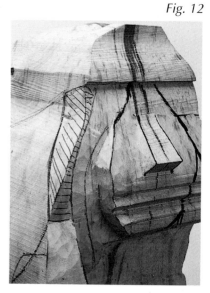

Fig. 11

Fig. 12

One more small area is removed, Fig. 12, and the face is accessible to start work on.

The first area to remove is all the front surface either side of the nose, mouth and chin, taking it back to the level of the front of the eyelids, Fig. 13. (See also Fig. 6). Where this runs up to the middle of the face the corners should be rounded with a gouge, not cut in square, Figs 14 and 15. The corners of the face resulting from this procedure can now be rounded, Fig. 15. Study the photos from below to get some idea of the shape you are working towards, Figs 20, 23, 26 and 29, and the cross sections, Fig. 7.

When the curved shape of the face has been established, the location of the eyes should be care-

Fig. 13

Fig. 14

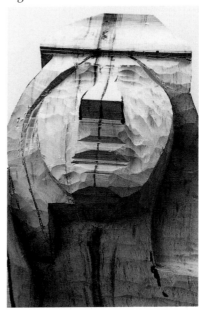

Fig. 15

Fig. 16

Fig. 17

fully measured and marked on as circles, Fig. 16. At this stage on a small head I find it easier to use a rotary burr rather than chisels. In this case, start with a 3mm ball shaped cutter, stroking the wood from side to side, Fig. 17. Using the burr, hollow out the areas round the eyeballs leaving them protruding as shallow domes. Particular attention must be paid to the inside and outside corners where there are deep recesses.

Next, move down to the wings of nose. Having measures the length of the nose from the tip to the backs of the nostrils, reduce the cheeks until you have achieved the correct length, Fig. 18. A smaller burr will be necessary in the tight curve around the nostrils.

The lips and chin can now be roughly shaped. The basic shape of the face should now be complete and appear as Fig. 19.

The burr can also be used to make the initial

Fig. 19
Fig. 20

Fig. 18

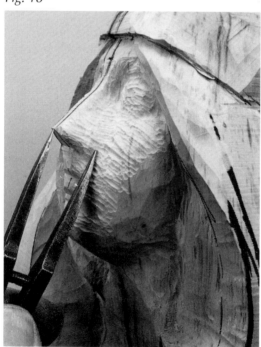

shaping of the upper eyelid. This will be made deeper than occurs naturally to compensate for the shadow created by lashes. Fig. 20 shows the eyelids roughed in from below. Check the symmetry and correctness of the shapes by looking up and down the face. Remember, if you do not do this, you are only working in two dimensions. After the eyelids are roughed in with the burr, they can be cut in with small shallow gouges and the spherical shape of the eyeball formed using a sharp pointed knife. Once this geometric shape is achieved it is relatively simple to fit the eyelids around it, Fig. 21.

Notice that the eyeball is tilted forward, so that the top lid is well in front of the bottom one. Also the top lid is undercut, sloping upwards and backwards underneath to create a dark shadow, while the bottom lid slopes forward, thus catching the light, Fig. 22.

Fig. 22

Fig. 23

Fig. 21

The lips are now shaped. First measure carefully from the bottom lid of each eye to the corresponding corner of the mouth, to ensure that they are parallel. The corners of the mouth will usually have to be brought back round the face because the mouth area will not be curved enough. This means that you must judge the distance 'G-G' Fig. 6, and round the mouth back to this point, at the same time maintaining the correct width. Check this against the cross section Fig. 7 and Fig. 26. The joint of the lips must be deeply cut, curvaceous, and the lips well rounded and full. At the corner there is a slight depression and all the surfaces roll into the corner — there should be no sharp lines. The area above the top lip is slightly hollowed so that the lips curl outward.

Very subtle shaping beneath the eyes, the cheekbones at the sides of the nose and round the chin are now necessary. On the boxwood carving shown I used a scraper for this but on a softer wood a riffler file or coarse abrasive could be used, Figs 25–29.

The iris can be cut in after the eyeball has been satisfactorily sanded to a perfectly smooth curve. Draw the iris on the eyeball, then, using a ball-ended burr, hollow the circle into a saucer shape, smoothing

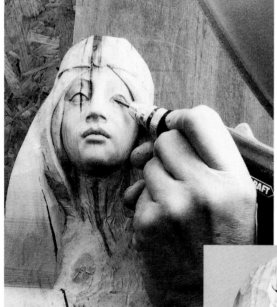

Fig. 24

Fig. 25

Fig. 26

this with a diamond burr (Fig 24). Next, drill a fairly deep hole for the pupil using a burr, enlarging it as required. The iris can be taken up under the top lid.

The face must now be sanded, starting with 80 grit and working through to 240. Do not start with a finer grit or you will end up with tool marks showing on the finished surface.

There are many finishes that can be used. I find that wax polish can easily clog up details on small scale work, and I usually use a satin picture varnish from a spray can.

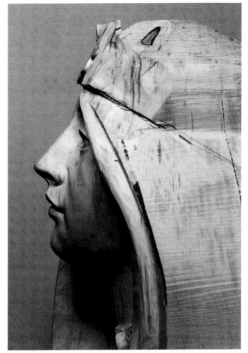

Fig. 28

Fig. 29

Fig. 27

3

THE EXPRESSIVE FACE

Having seen an example of a passive expression, and how it is created, we will now study the practical application on a small scale, carving a more expressive example. Most carvers will be working on figures up to 60cm (24") high which means that the face will only be 5 or 7.5cm (2" or 3") high, possibly smaller. It is all the more important to understand the basic mechanics of the face in order that the main, significant forms are put in place — the lengthening of the jaw when the mouth opens, the thickening of the cheeks when grinning — if these major shapes are correctly formed initially, the smaller details tend to fall easily into place.

The best approach to carving a head like this is to find a person prepared to pose holding the expression while you take photographs. This is cheap and easy to do, and I find most people quite willing. Take pictures from all angles, not forgetting from above and below. Study your model and your photos, relating them to the anatomy drawings in order to understand what is happening under the skin (Figs 1–3). Make a clay model, prior to carving, not in full detail but just blocking out the main masses of the face. I can not stress enough that you must start with real reference material. For example, if you wish to copy a picture in a magazine or book, take your own photos of a similar model, to supplement the information you have.

In this study, photographs of one model were used in conjunction with drawings of another. The face is intended to express hope and exhilaration, but with just a trace of worry, of someone trying to achieve something wonderful that is probably beyond them. The head is carved in walnut and is 4.5cm (1 ¾") from the eyebrows to the point of the chin.

In the drawings and photographs, Figs 30–35, it will be seen that the eyebrows are raised as high as possible by the frontalis muscle on the forehead, in order to assist the eyelids to open wide for better vision. The mouth is open, partly to take in extra breath for the exertion of leaping, and partly drawing back at the corners, in a grin. This draws the muscle around the mouth tightly around the teeth, hollows the cheeks as the jaw opens, and creates deeply stretched lines from the nose to the chin. Some thickening and wrinkling is created under the eyes, as is normal with a grin. A trace of worry is shown by slight creases between the eyebrows. It can be seen in Fig. 40 that when these creases are not present the face looks quite happy.

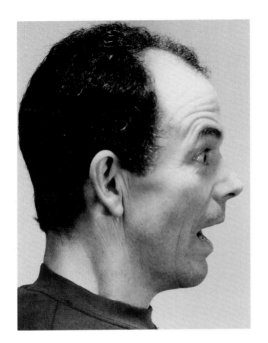

Figs 30–31

Figs 32–33

Figs 34–35

Taking up the carving from a situation where the basic form of the head has been roughed out, Fig. 36, a centre line has been drawn down the nose, and the eye, mouth and main deep furrows of the face marked in on the left side. On the right side these features have been carved creating the hollowing of the eye sockets with a slight bulge for the eyeball. The cheekbone starts to show as a result of cutting in the infra-orbital furrow and slightly hollowing the cheek. The naso-labial furrows have been roughed in forming the curve of the mouth, which has then been indicated. Virtually all of this work has been carried out using rotary burrs rather than gouges, which on this small scale, should be found to be easier. This stage can be seen from the side in Fig. 37.

Fig. 36

Fig. 37

Fig. 38

Fig. 39

Fig. 40

In Fig. 38, the nose has been developed, the nostrils flared and pulled up at an angle by the retracted cheek muscle. Notice that the mouth has been turned up at the corner creating more of a smile, which in Fig. 36 appears more as a grimace. The furrows at the sides of the mouth have been deepened, bringing the chin to more of a point, and the mouth hollowed out slightly.

At this point you should find it best to roughly sand the face and check that all is symmetrical before starting on detail. On this scale any imbalances in the basic shape will be hard to correct. Viewing the head from below, above and in the mirror, will help to show up inaccuracies.

The eyes are now cut in with small gouges in the usual way. The eyeballs should be sanded before completing the lids or they may be damaged, Fig. 39.

Moving down the face, Fig. 40, the nose and cheekbones are refined using riffler files and abrasives. The nostrils are drilled out with a burr and the opening of the mouth deepened. The teeth are cut in and separated from the lips. The lips are very thin and tightly stretched around the teeth.

Fig. 41

In Fig. 41 the forehead corrugations are formed using a knife to cut a deep line and then rounding off with a small flat gouge. The wrinkles under the eyes are made with a small 'u' shaped gouge. The desired expression is now beginning to appear. In the finished head, Figs 42, 43 and 44, this is enhanced by the irises which reveal the fact that the eyes are looking upward, thereby explaining the furrowed brow and the deepening of the hollows at each side of the mouth. The furrows in the cheeks are sharply defined to create more tension in the jaw.

In comparing the finished head with the original drawings, various differences can be seen. The corners of the mouth have been raised and deepened slightly to make more of a smile. For the same reason, the cheeks have been pushed upwards as they do when the mouth forms a grin. Finally, the eyebrows have been raised to create a more alert and hopeful look. The finished carving is shown in Fig. 45.

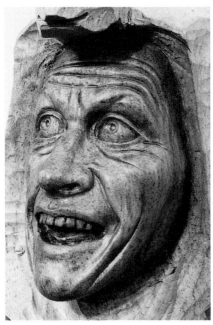

Fig. 42

Fig. 43   Fig. 44

Fig. 45

Carvings, unless they are portraits, are not intended to look like individual people — they are creations, and the carver's job is to put what he wants into his creation. Therefore when the live model does not fulfil your requirements, you make up the shortcomings. A model can not be expected to show real surprise, joy, pain, etc, so amendments and exaggerations must be made. Usually it is not difficult to open the eyes a little wider by cutting back the lids, to add a laughter line or raise an eyebrow. These small details will raise your carving above the average by putting your personal touch into it.

4

THE EXAGGERATED EXPRESSION

The next carving shows a man concentrating intensely, his tongue poking from the corner of his mouth, frowning, eyes staring. What he is actually doing is trying to sew a hole in a sock, the reason being that the theatre dresser has departed. In this unaccustomed situation, Harlequin is frustrated by his own incompetence at this simple task. The expression may seem extreme, but if you study people performing even the simplest tasks, the pursed lips, the frowns, the biting of lips and the poking of tongues are often out of all proportion to the difficulty of the operation. Others, for instance musicians, maintain the most bland, distracted expressions whilst performing extremely complex tasks. What I feel you must aim for is the archetypal expression in order to convey to the observer the point you are making. If Harlequin looked as if he sewed his socks every day, the point would be lost, so the expression must be obvious. More subtle expressions are obviously desirable at times, but they must be clearly subtle — the trace of a frown must be clearly seen to be just that.

Figs 46–47

Figs 48 and 49 show the early stages of the carving, the eyebrows pulled down into a permanent shelf, the nostrils flared and pulled slightly upward, the cheeks drawn, showing up the cheekbones and deeply scarred naso-labial furrows, which virtually isolate the mouth area from the rest of the face. From Fig. 49 it can be seen that the side of the mouth where the tongue pokes out is drawn back considerably from the other side.

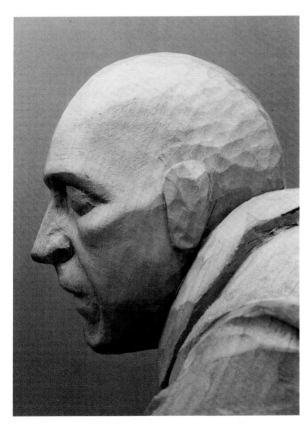

Fig. 48

Fig. 49

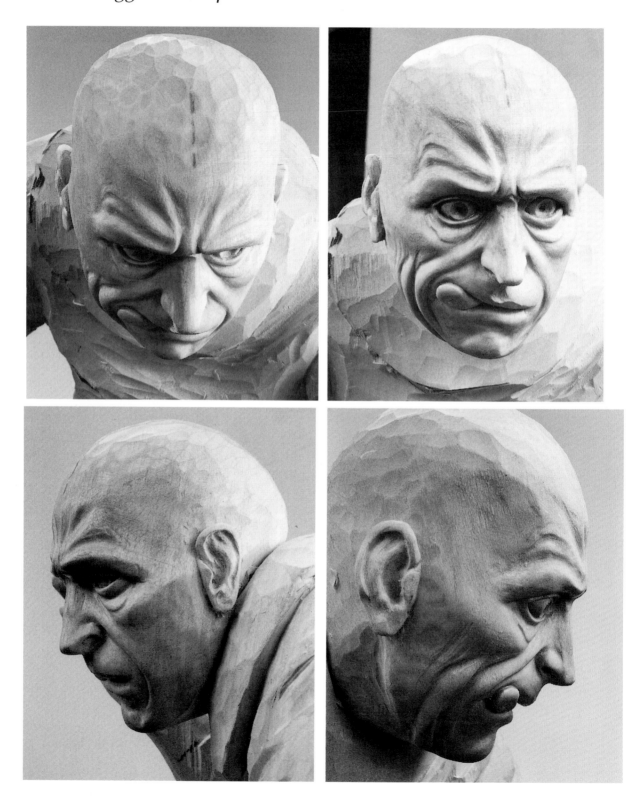

Figs 50 to 53 show the deep folding of the cheek formed by this action in contrast with the more tightly stretched opposite cheek. The forehead is deeply furrowed and drawn in towards the centre. The lines of the face focus our attention on the eyes, which are wide open and staring, re-directing our attention to the object of his gaze. What makes the stare so intense is the contradictory nature of the expression. Normally, a frown of concentration would indicate screwed up or half closed eyes. The wide open stare contradicts this and is therefore unusual. Although more natural I feel the half closed eyes would suggest a greater degree of confidence whilst the staring eyes seem to suggest a frustration bordering on madness.

However that may be, it is certain that tiny changes in the face will affect it greatly.

Notice also that the face is not actually very detailed. Only major features are carved — large folds of skin, prominent furrows and forms. There are no small wrinkles and folds to confuse the situation — the face is in fact simplified and stylised like a mask.

The main point is that you must decide on the expression you want and do everything to enhance it. Imagine for a moment that Harlequin's eyebrows were raised high instead of being lowered. The face would then become a simple-minded Stan Laurel type of character. Once you understand the face, tricks like this can be played to your advantage.

Opposite, Figs 50–53

5

RANGE OF EXPRESSIONS

RELAXED

Compare the face in Fig. 54 with the facial features diagram Fig. 3.

From the side the frontal eminencies and brow ridges can be clearly seen. On the man's face these are far less distinct, although typically, the reverse is true. Although the infra-orbital furrow can be seen on the female (Figs 56 and 57), the tear bags can not, but these are highly developed on the man. Also the eye cover fold on the man is sagging over the upper lid. The bone at the bridge of the nose is not apparent on the girl, Fig. 57, but very marked on the man. Notice that although the naso-labial furrow and mouth angle

Fig. 54

Fig. 55

furrow particularly, can be seen on the girl, they are rounded forms, whilst on the man they have become fixed lines. However, the man's lips and philtrum have lost all definition compared to the girl's. Overall, the young female face is soft and rounded, whereas the older man's is linear and incised. It is this that makes older faces so much easier to carve, and give them character.

The carved head shown here Fig. 58, from 'The Idealist' is 10cm (4") high and intended to be expressionless to show the subject's indifference to the world around him. The face has been made thin to indicate his ascetic way of life and the eyes are blind because his world is internal not external. However, the deep furrows and slightly downturned mouth suggest a touch of bitterness at society's neglect of his great ideals.

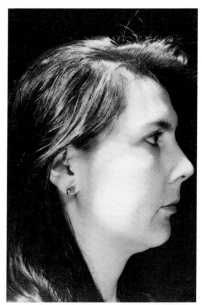 

Figs 56–57

Fig. 58

HAPPY

Referring now to the same people smiling, it is re-markable how similar the facial reactions are in two very different people — the heavy crinkling under and at the corners of the eyes and the deepening of the naso-labial furrows. Another furrow appears on both, running from below the chin, up the cheek. This can be seen in an extreme form in Fig. 64. It should be clear from these pictures that the common practice of cutting lines in the face with a 'V' tool is totally inadequate and inappropriate. These folds are either soft and smooth or deep with sharply rounded edges. Nowhere is there a 'V'. One could conceiv-ably use it for the creases on the man's forehead but the edges would have to be rounded.

The muscles radiating from the mouth are con-tracting and pulling the lips upwards and backwards. There is also some contraction of the circular muscle round the eye. This clearly demonstrates the folding of the skin created at right angles to the direction of the muscle contraction.

Figs 59–60

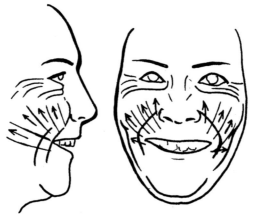

Fig. 61

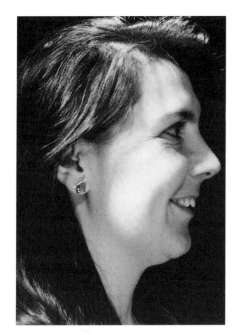 

Figs 62–63

Fig. 64

These studies show a grinning face carved in walnut, Fig. 65, and a grinning devil's mask, Fig. 66. Neither of these faces seem to express genuine pleasure but rather one of evil delight or sadistic pleasure. This is because the faces are frowning at the same time as smiling, which is a contradictory situation. If you cover the top half of the face Fig. 64, the smile is quite natural and, conversely, by covering the bottom half you have a typical frowning face.

The photograph of the model Fig. 67 shows an appearance similar to Fig. 64, an expression which he considered to be aggressive but which may not appear so to others. What this seems to tell us about facial expressions is that they are an interpretation of the perceived emotional situation. Taken out of context they can be misinterpreted. It follows, therefore, that on a carving which may not be in context the facial expression must be made obvious by exaggeration or at least making it patently clear what is intended.

Fig. 88, for example, shows Shylock at the moment of his being denounced in court. Like the exaggerated photographs of the model he displays stereotyped symptoms of suspicion, fear, anger and hate all vying for dominance. The heavy frown, sidelong look, drawn face and down-stretched mouth all contribute to this end.

Fig. 65

Fig. 66

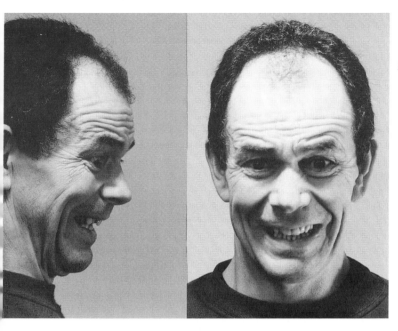

Fig. 67

The young boy, Figs 68 and 69, is a 'natural' smiler. Notice the excessive corrugations of the cheeks at the sides of the nose, the thickening of the lower lids and cheeks.

Figs 68–69

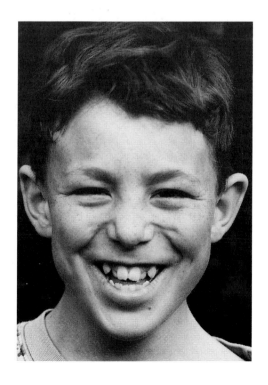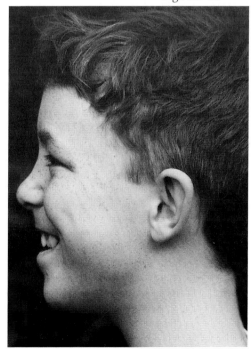

In the face of Falstaff, Fig. 70, these reactions are the only signs we see behind the facial hair but it is enough for us to read his character. In the satyr's face Fig. 71, we have the contradictory signs — the grinning mouth, the heavy frown and the staring eyes. As mentioned before, these unnatural combinations of expressions tend to create bizarre or disturbing effects, and here perhaps is the 'lascivious' rather than the 'jolly' shown in Falstaff.

Fig. 72 shows an oriental mask where the symptoms of laughing are greatly exaggerated, but so is the frown — is he laughing or screaming? Compare this with the young girl in Fig. 73. Notice the perfect symmetry of her lineless face exuding innocent *joie de vivre*.

Fig. 70

Fig. 71

Fig. 72

Figs 73–74

SADNESS

These two studies, Figs 75 and 77, are quite fascinating in their display of subtle muscular interplay. On both subjects the eyes are so hooded they seem to have sunk in to the skull as if to hide from the awful truth. The foreheads are distorted, but notice that the movement is not symmetrical, particularly on the older man where one side goes up and the other one down. However, the mouth area is most expressive where the nodes have been pulled downwards, in turn stretching and hollowing the cheeks, giving the face a drawn look. The chin boss has moved upward pushing against the bottom lips creating a deep fold between them. Deep lines and folds are formed at the bottom of the cheek. The whole becomes almost comical as you study it.

Figs 75–76

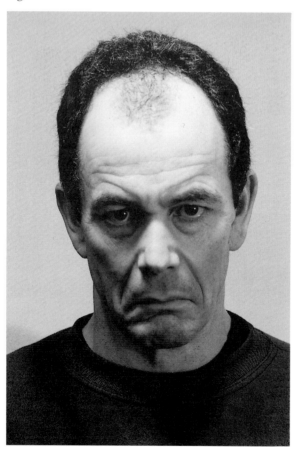
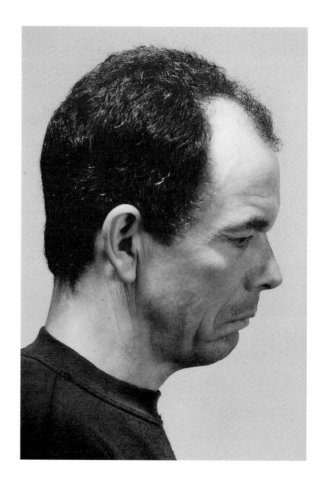

Figs 77–78

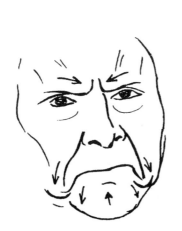 

In the carving, Fig. 79, although the top half of the face is covered by the mask, the mouth area is similar to those in the photographs and the expression is basically the same. The eyes, however, do not appear as hooded as the models, suggesting that the lines around the mouth are a permanent fixture showing a sour nature.

The important point for this carving is that the mouth is the more expressive part of the face. If the top half of the model's face is covered, the lower half is still miserable, whereas the reverse is not so, the eyes alone tending to look rather evil and could well be used in another carving where that look was required. Your model must pose with the required expression, but as will be seen in several photographs in this book, the model's idea of an expression of a particular emotion and how it appears in a photo are not necessarily the same. You must create the expression so that it is obvious to all. If you wish to add details such as masks, helmets, beards and so on, you must ensure that the expression is still apparent when these are in place.

Fig. 79

ANGER

Figs 80 and 81 show the face of aggression in which every muscle seems to be tense — even the platysma of the neck (known as the harp strings). The whole structure of the face is changed and the meaning is quite unequivocal. The teeth are bared ready for fighting and the face contorted to frighten the enemy. Great care must be taken carving a face like this or it will look ridiculous, particularly the teeth which must be accurately and precisely cut, not left like a row of tombstones.

Figs 80–81

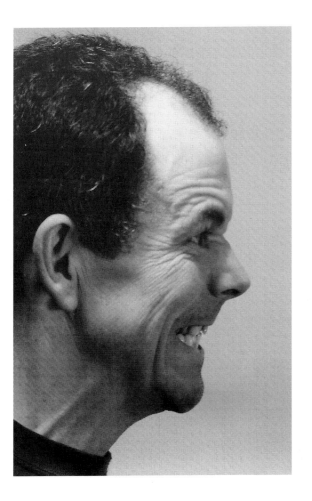

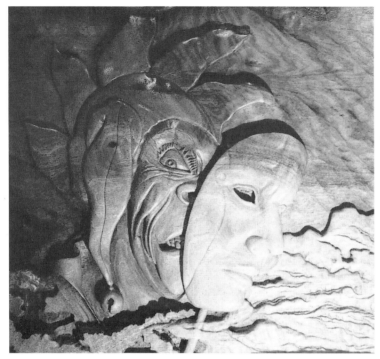

Fig. 82 (Detail from Marillion)

Fig. 84 shows a variety of angry faces. They all exhibit the same characteristics, which can be seen in the carvings Figs 82 and 83.

Fig. 83 (Detail from The Box of Delights)

Fig. 84

ENVY

Figs 85, 86, 87 and 88 are my rather theatrical ideas
of envy, but they might also be interpreted as suspicion, fear, anger or hate. These emotions are complex and related — no doubt one who is extremely
envious may be suspicious of the object of the envy,
may hate him and be filled with anger. In such cases
one must try to emphasise the significance of the
facial expression by the use of body language, perhaps a clenched fist clutching some object to the
body like Shylock, Fig. 88.

Figs 85–86

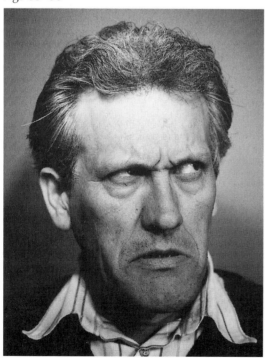 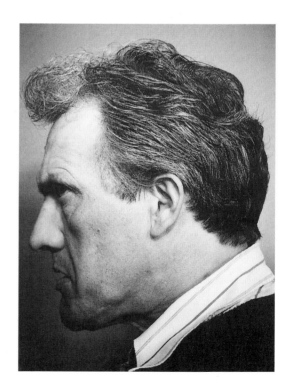

Fig. 87 (Detail from Box of Delights)

Fig. 88 Shylock

FEAR

Fear is caused by many different stimuli from the fear of losing your money to the fear of imminent death and its expression will also be varied. In some cases people would clench their teeth and screw up their eyes to shut out some awful things, Figs 89 and 90; others would open their eyes wide in horror and scream, Figs 91 and 92. The boxwood statuette in the Victoria & Albert Museum entitled 'Fear' shows a face with wide eyes, a slight frown and moderately open mouth. Taken alone it could be someone singing or calling out, but the tense stance, the disarrayed hair and the violent folds in the clothing all add to the impression of fear or at least fright. Nevertheless, this 18th century carver placed a hare on the base of the carving because his audience would immediately understand that it symbolised timidity and fearfulness.

Although one might interpret Fig. 89 as pain or disgust and Fig. 92 as surprise or shock, are these not part of the emotions of fear? This would range for instance from the realisation that there was smoke in your bedroom through the horror of seeing the flames, to the scream of terror as you leapt from the window. In different scenarios the faces would be different.

The carving, Fig. 93, shows a caricatured version of Fig. 92 with bulging eyes and open mouth. The three heads are in fact looking down at some rather unseemly goings on below them and showing their different reaction to it.

Figs 89–90

Figs 91–92

Fig. 93

ROGUES GALLERY

Clearly there are an infinite number of faces and variations of expression. To record the second by second changes in one person's face would need a motion picture and all we have is a few photographs of individuals trying to express emotions they do not even feel at the time, and which often do not appear to suggest that emotion to other people. Where does that leave us then? What we can do is to learn the simple mechanics of the face and the psychology that relates to it, and then use it to our own advantage, just as the makers of masks and gargoyles did in the past and make-up artists still do.

The following pages show a variety of faces and expressions, some of which have been used in carvings. I suggest that you use every opportunity to photograph faces and collect them from magazines, etc, to create your own rogues gallery.

NOBILITY

Artists have been trying to portray a look of nobility for thousands of years. When one looks at some of the Greek statues of Apollo, it seems that either we have not progressed very much, or that there is a look which is recognisably 'noble' or 'superior'.

It is usually portrayed by a slightly raised head, the slightest suggestion of a frown, a thickening of the lower eyelid and a faraway look in the eyes. Overall the impression is of a totally immobile face, as if to say 'I am in control', and an intense cat-like stare at some distant point.

Fig. 94   Slave girl

Fig. 95   Zamburu woman

In Fig. 94, I have attempted to portray dignity and strength in adversity. It is interesting that the face of the Zamburu woman, Fig. 95, has almost exactly the same look, but was carved with completely different intent, several years later.

The Masai warrior Fig. 96 and Ozymandias, the Egyptian king, Fig. 97, have similar expressions. The model in Figs 98 and 99 gives an indication of the slightly raised head mentioned earlier.

The Alchemist, Fig. 100, is intended to show his belief in his own superiority by reason of his magical skills.

Study of antique Greek, Egyptian, Roman and Renaissance art would be well repaid in the search for nobility.

Fig. 96   Masai warrior

Fig. 97   Ozymandias

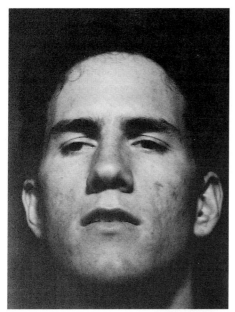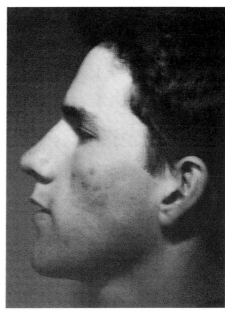

Figs 98–99

Fig. 100   The Alchemist

DETERMINATION

Fig. 101 depicts the Gallic warrior Vercingetorix immediately prior to being executed by the victorious Roman general. The jaws are tightly clenched and the bottom lip pushed out pugnaciously, perhaps to stop his teeth chattering. Again, taken in context, the carving works quite well, whilst the photographs of the model, Figs 102 and 103, at first appear rather comical. If you cover the face from the lips down, the model has a most definite determined look — the eyes tell us that nothing is going to get in the way of the decision which has been made. Fig. 104 is a slight variation on Fig. 103 but with a 'do your worst' look, caused by tiny changes in the face. This shows the value of having several different studies to work from. Pick the most expressive features you think necessary to give your carving the feel that it needs to succeed.

Fig. 101

Figs 102–103 & 104

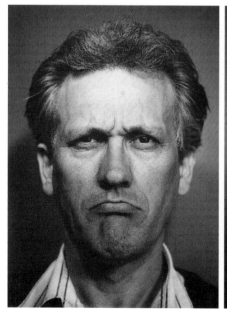  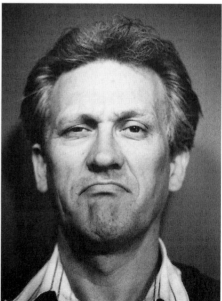

Figs 105–106

Fig. 107

WORKING FACES

Figs 105 and 106 showing a boy blowing a flute were used to create the ugly character in Fig. 107 blowing bubbles. In truth I do not think people puff out their cheeks to blow flutes or bubbles but I felt it was a more expressive face than the real thing. Fig. 105 is an excellent picture — notice how the raised eyebrows and furrowed brow, the slightly closed eyes, the top lip pressed against the nose, the muscles in the neck and even the quiff of hair all seem to contribute to the feeling of blowing. Fig. 106 is not so expressive because the boy has become self-conscious, looking at the photographer.

In my carving I have exaggerated the eyebrows and bony ridges above the eyes. The cheeks are more defined than on the boy and the features are generally coarser and more pronounced as one would

Fig. 108

expect on an older person. This is a useful expression which could be adapted for a variety of figures such as a cherub, a musician or something more comical.

Fig. 108 shows the head of a fool sniffing a flower, the expression exaggerated to the point of being ridiculous. And Figs 109 and 110 are equally odd faces and continue the sniffing or smelling theme. These may be rarely required, but there is an increasing interest carving caricatures and a portfolio of silly, action faces could easily provide the springboard for ideas for future work.

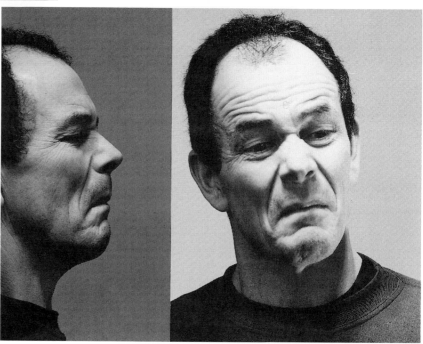

Figs 109–110

CHARACTER

Character in faces is a rather elusive thing to pin down. We all know when we see a face with 'character' but to determine what actually creates character in a face is not so easy. If it is simply an attribute of ageing, that is to say, wrinkles, then it is rather meaningless. In Fig. 111 there are several faces with wrinkles, the two at top right caused simply by living in a harsh environment. The clown at the bottom is able to pull grotesque faces but the expressions have no meaning for us, whereas the man at the bottom left pulling a 'facial shrug', at least seems to give us an impression of his character.

The oriental lady looks as if she would be a bit of a joker. The downward smile is curious — one has to cover the entire face except for the mouth, before the mouth becomes unhappy — as it should). But the old boy at top left has, I think, what most people would call a bit of character in his face. Whether this is simply a stereotype is hard to say. I think there is something about the eyes, the left one being slightly more closed, as if he were winking at us, the slight cock-eyed smile and the forehead wrinkled on one side giving a slightly quizzical look that makes us warm to this face — one could build a whole character around the face. Yet for all we know he could be a monster. However, these philosophical problems are not our prime concern. If we need to carve a face with 'character' we are faced with reproducing minute variations of facial characteristics which can vanish as quickly as a mood changes.

A good source of the right faces I think would be actors and actresses whose faces are their fortune. Look at a lot of the type of character you require and analyse what are the features that make them so and concentrate on those in your carving, emphasising a slight quirk of the mouth or hooding of the eye.

The actual carving of heavily lined faces such as these requires considerable technical expertise. The folds can be very deep and acute. If you clench your fist and study the fold around your forefinger you will see the effect I mean. Deep, clean cutting is needed which you may find is best done with a very sharp knife which will cut deeply without much side pressure. Two cuts at an acute angle should release the sliver of wood and the corners can then be carefully rounded. 'V' tools are useless for this. As the creases become smaller, shallower and more numerous such as the forehead of the man at centre right, a very small veiner might be used. The problem is that ultimately one ends up with a face that has many folds, but the general surface of the wood is still smooth, whilst the skin is actually textured. On occasion, in the case of exceptionally wrinkled skin I have covered the entire surface in a network of fine gouge cuts. Using a fine punch may be worth trying. It also depends on the scale of the head. Ultimately one must accept the limitations of the medium.

(Fig. 111 over page)

SUBTLE EXPRESSIONS

If expressions must be obvious and unambiguous, where does that leave us with the more subtle expressions, which after all are probably more useful than extreme ones?

The face on Touchstone, Fig. 112, is my interpretation of the Shakespearean character — a court jester who is intelligent, witty, somewhat cynical and jaded, but basically generous.

With such a complex character, the expressions must be complex and subtle, and if it is ambiguous, well that is the nature of the character. Notice also the slightly smug smile on the face of Merlin, Fig. 113, and that in contrast to the face in Fig. 64, the eyebrows are raised appropriately for the smile. This creates a rather bland, unworried and nonchalant look which we tend to associate with someone who is rather pleased with themselves.

Fig. 112   Touchstone

Fig. 113   Merlin

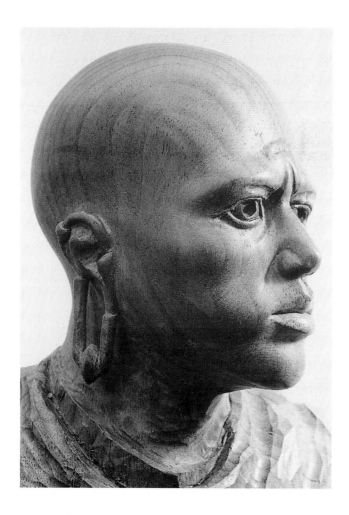

Fig. 114   Masai warrior

Fig. 115   Jester

The traces of concern on the Masai warrior's face, Fig. 114, indicated by the slight furrowing of the forehead and the rather tight lips, show that a minimal amount of carving can create a subtle expression. Fig. 115 shows the jester peering from behind a mask — What is he thinking? — perhaps he is ashamed of being laughed at, or just got stage fright. The lines on the forehead are somewhat stylised, but this is in keeping with the whole figure and is reminiscent of theatrical make up.

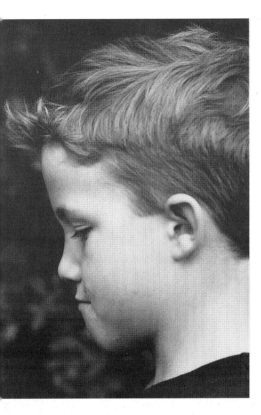 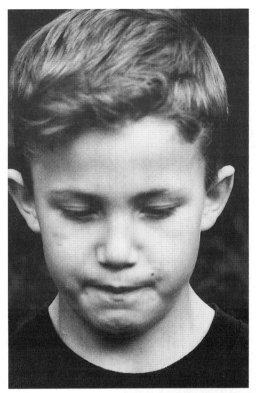

Figs 116 and 117 show a boy looking sad or perhaps pensive — not really unhappy. Fig. 118 shows 'The Stripper' with much the same expression but people feel she is sad, I suppose because they imagine a stripper should be sad.

Fig. 118

Figs 119–120

The face of the teenage girl, Figs 119 and 120 shows the protruding bottom lip, also detectable on the boy, which was mentioned previously in relation to determination, Fig. 103. There is also something of the same feeling on the Masai warrior's face Fig. 114. This feature obviously strikes a chord in us, signifying a holding back of strong, unhappy emotions. Notice the complete lack of facial line on the younger face. The muscles are still working but as yet have not developed sufficiently to pull the face into creases.

Figs 121 and 122 show some of the subtle yet powerful expressions created by slight facial changes.

The eyebrows are major players in the expression of moods. They are very mobile and are capable of minute variations which can usually be interpreted as an indication of the person's state of mind. Fig. 121 shows some subtle expressions, not necessarily identifiable specifically, but in a certain category one might call 'troubled'. The young face at the top is the almost indifferent but the slight droopiness round the mouth suggests a certain despondency. On a young face these shapes must be very soft and can be achieved simply by judicious sanding in the appropriate areas. The middle face is definitely a little bitter around the mouth, but the eyebrows are heading for a frown. There is also a hollowing under the eyes and in the cheeks which seems to appear when people are under stress. The sculptor Bernini accentuated the hollowing under the eyes on his marble to simulate the slight blue colouring often seen there which makes the face appear sunken eyed. The lower right face certainly has a problem, which if you cover the mouth, is independent of the rest of the face. It is all in the slight creases between the brows and the lowering of them which makes the eyes appear so sunken. These expressions, particularly the eyebrows, must be prepared for in the roughing out stage. If a normal, open-eyed, raised eyebrow is carved the upper lid is more visible and the space above it curving upward. When the brow is lowered and like an overhanging shelf, a very different shape must be allowed.

Clearly this is seen in Fig. 122 where the woman on the left has one raised eyebrow. Compare the space above the eye within the two male faces. In the face, lower right, the eyes are very reduced in aperture with much thickening of the lids and the surrounding areas. The normal process of carving an eye hardly applies here. The eyeball, normally a high point, here becomes the lowest point in a mass of crumpled skin.

In Fig. 84, faces of anger, there are some quite extraordinary contortions of the brow area. These must be carved very carefully in order to be convincing rather than artificially theatrical. No 'V' tools will suffice — the skin must be carefully modelled to show the rounded swelling forms created by extreme muscular activity. These are not grooves on smooth surfaces, but corrugations of a surface. Fine work with knife and chisels, followed perhaps by rifler files and sanding are required.

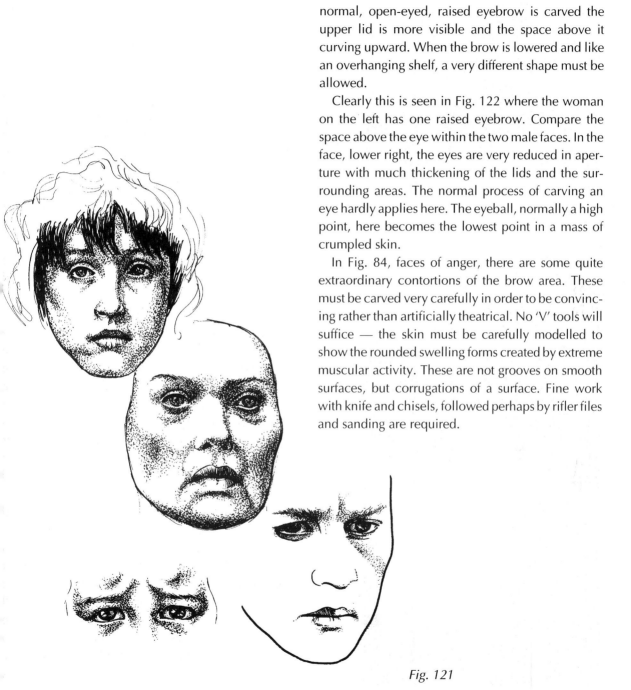

Fig. 121

Fig. 122

6

WORKING EXAMPLES

Having studied the range of human expression in some depth we will now look at two examples of how to utilise the information in the book. The first carving is of a woman who has just been responsible for the murder of her former lover with a spear. She is holding the spear and looking up at the point. Within the 4.5cm (1¾") high head one must try to show an appropriate expression. There is no need to be too specific — we do not really know what she thinks, but assuming she is not gloating or congratulating herself, one would expect tenseness, concern, perhaps anxiety at the consequences, regret. To a large extent these subtle emotions are interpreted by the audience in their own way, in the context of the whole carving. Surely this is one of the pleasures of owning a work of art.

The face used is that of a professional model having no particular expression. This has then been altered in Fig. 123 by using details from other faces in the book. The small creases between the eyebrows are taken from the bald headed man in Fig. 122, but without the heavy frown. The eyes are large and fully open, looking up at the spear as if with child-like innocence or mystification, but are still fairly heavy-lidded to give a rather dull sad look. They are also well hollowed below, giving an unhealthy, tired look, emphasised by the hollowing of the cheeks. These details were taken from the woman in Fig. 121, the mouth was also altered to resemble this face, by drawing down the corners and slightly emphasising the lines at the corners.

This example shows that it is not difficult to alter faces. If, for example, one changed the eyes on this figure for lowered ones, such as Figs 116 and 118, the impression given would be much more one of remorse, the murderess being unable to look at the weapon and retreating into herself.

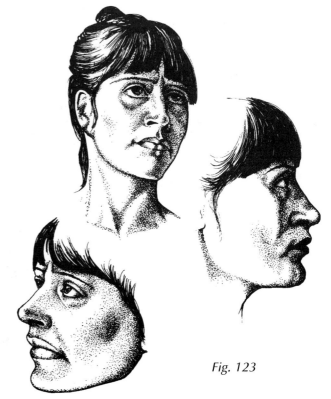

Fig. 123

You may well feel that at the moment you are technically unequipped to carve details on faces of this size accurately enough to capture these expressions. Nevertheless, you should be trying to from day one. Your face will certainly be no better for lack of expression.

Starting with the bandsawn figure Fig. 124, the first thing to do is to realign the head from its straight forward position to one turned slightly to the side. This is not easy and must be done most carefully on this small scale, to avoid irredeemable errors. Work looking down on the head, Fig. 125. Remember that if you only look at the front and side you are working in two dimensions only. You must constantly look up the face and down it, or you will never achieve perfect symmetry in it. Fig. 126 shows the carving roughed out with the gouges. More detail of the main masses of the face are then worked using a 3mm ball ended burr, Fig. 127. A smaller burr is used on the lips, nostrils and in the corners of the eyes. Notice that the modelling around the lips, the hollowing of the cheeks, the eyebrows and naso-labial furrows are well established. Using a couple of ball-ended diamond burrs the shapes are refined. The lines at the corner of the mouth are introduced, the cheekbone shape and the whole face smoothed so that the forms can be more easily read. The division of the lips and the edges of the nostrils are cut in with chisels. The final details now drop into place relatively easily because the groundwork has been done carefully. The eyes are cut in, the little furrows on the forehead and the lips given more definition, Fig. 128.

This is now a rather hard, sour-looking face. As I described it in my earlier book, 'Fundamentals of Figure Carving', the face, particularly that of a young woman, requires considerable fine and careful sanding, almost to the point of obliterating the details so carefully carved, to produce the desired youthful look. Fig. 129 shows the progression of this stage.

Figs 124–126

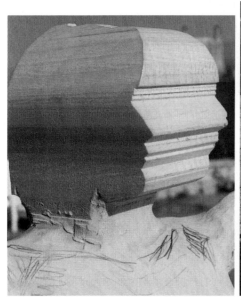

Figs 127–129

Fig. 130

The second example is the head of a jester who is supposed to look like a happy, good-natured type. The figure is in walnut and the head is 4.5cm (1¾") high. Figs 130 and 131 show the face roughed out with gouges, the main forms in place. Notice the shadows under the cheeks where the mouth is to be pulled back in a big smile.

In Fig. 132, the left-hand side of the face has been worked on with a burr shaping the eye socket and the nostril, the lips and the deep crease on the cheek. On the right-hand side these details have been enhanced with burrs and gouges. The eye has been cut in and the lips shaped. The deep fold at the sides of the mouth are taken from the boy in Figs 68 and 69,

Figs 131–133

including the relatively unusual creases running outward from the nostrils. When the other side of the
face was completed the head looked as in Fig. 133. I
felt this had a rather wistful look about it, not really
the feeling I wanted. The raised eyebrow on one side
was taken from the bald, bearded man in Fig. 111,
and this contributed to the wrong look. I therefore
took more details from the old man in Fig. 111,
deepening the creases under the eyes and slightly
accentuating the forehead furrows. Still not satisfied,
I then referred to the smiling face in Figs 59 and 60
and added more deep creases at the corners of the
eyes, rounded the cheeks more and deepened the
lines from nose to chin. I also made a slight opening
in the mouth. If I could have opened the lips more as
in Fig. 59, I would have done so, as I feel this is the
root of the problem. A person who smiles with their
lips firmly sealed never appears to be really letting
go. However, the end result, Fig. 134, is satisfactory.

Fig. 134